THE COVID-19 MONSTER UNDER MY BED
A DIARY

SCOTT GOODYER

Copyright © 2020 Scott Goodyer.

All rights reserved. No part of this book may be reproduced, stored, or transmitted by any means—whether auditory, graphic, mechanical, or electronic—without written permission of the author, except in the case of brief excerpts used in critical articles and reviews. Unauthorized reproduction of any part of this work is illegal and is punishable by law.

This is a work of fiction. All of the characters, names, incidents, organizations, and dialogue in this novel are either the products of the author's imagination or are used fictitiously.

ISBN: 978-1-7167-4084-8 (sc)
ISBN: 978-1-7167-4083-1 (e)

Because of the dynamic nature of the Internet, any web addresses or links contained in this book may have changed since publication and may no longer be valid. The views expressed in this work are solely those of the author and do not necessarily reflect the views of the publisher, and the publisher hereby disclaims any responsibility for them.

Any people depicted in stock imagery provided by Getty Images are models, and such images are being used for illustrative purposes only. Certain stock imagery © Getty Images.

Lulu Publishing Services rev. date: 08/21/2020

For those who washed their hands.

Day 1
March 13th, 2020

I SLIPPED ON my joggers again this morning wondering, *who the hell am I?*

A bird on a tree branch turned its head and whispered to me, "Don't touch your face." I look back into a mirror. The bird is my reflection, smiling back at me.

What am I going to do with all this toilet paper in my walls?

Randomly called a phone number. A stranger picked up. Told me some story about driving over a bridge but I hung up before they could finish.

The sun is now setting and the entire sky is pink. I think I know what I'll do with all that toilet paper now. Maybe if I toss it into the sky it'll fly away. Fly straight into that pink sky.

Day 2

IS IT JUST me or are you also waking up each morning to different stray cats staring at you in your bed?

I keep forgetting to lock my door.

Ventured out to a ransacked Costco this afternoon to buy some cat food. Instead of a membership card, I gave the masked lady my library card. She asked if she could keep it and I said yes. She said she always wanted to read some books about travelling to space.

When I got home, I thought about what it would be like to travel with her. Holding hands, we float among a sea of infinite stars surrounded by the cold, black abyss. We are behind Neptune when she finally takes her mask off for me.

We share a can of cat food.

Day 3

CLEANED OUT MY bedroom closet and found an old childhood book on face painting.

Canadian Prime Minister Justin Trudeau hops out of his Ottawa house to give a COVID-19 media update with a painted bunny face.

The book was written and illustrated in the early 80s by a grandfather who lived in Italy. I googled him and found out he died in 2002.

Made copies of the pages from the book and mailed them to random people feeling caged in isolation. Soon, everyone with a painted wolf face will gather in the city park at midnight.

The louder you howl, the stronger you feel.

Day 4

MY FIVE-YEAR-OLD NEPHEW video-called me today. He asked me how I was holding up. Making sure I had all the video games I needed.

My nephew's name is Jack. He's smart, handsome and courageous.

I told him that if you stare at a bottle of Purell long enough, you start to have actual flashes of the distant future.

When Jack grows up, he's going to be a real-life superhero in a post-apocalyptic world. Busting down doors, making sure everyone has enough toilet paper.

At the end of our video call, he told me his birthday is coming up.

As the frantic sound of police sirens blared past my apartment, I wondered what his wish would be when he blows out the candles on his Spider-Man cake.

Day 5

THE CITY IS empty except for a pack of travelling UberEats bicycle couriers. I've placed my order and tracked them through the streets.

Speeding along to techno music, their hearts beat as one.

The leader is dressed in colourful feathers, a bucket of chicken wings strapped to his back. The rest follow behind, jumping off curbs and parked cars.

Eventually, they disappear off my radar. I look out my window, up into the midnight sky.

But all I see is the sparkling full moon, shaped like my burger.

Day 6

MY FOUR-FOOT IKEA plant is not doing well. It's starting to yellow, curl up and dropping to the floor.

I took it to the hospital but because it hasn't lost any leaves, they refused to test it.

I almost didn't buy it when I first saw it at Ikea. My cart was full and I wanted an ice cream cone. But I figured I could use some more life in my tiny apartment.

If my plant dies, who knows how long I'll have to wait until I can get a new one.

I return to Ikea as an old man. Remember me? So, while I patiently wait in isolation, I go back to watching Netflix with my dying plant.

And ice cream all over my face.

Day 7

MY FAVOURITE THING to do right now is the grocery store run.

Our local store manager recently got sick and has been replaced. The new guy is 100% organic and was raised on a local farm. His name tag says Doug.

Every morning, the teenage employees gather in the back of the store and watch him lay eggs.

After your groceries are bagged, Doug personally offers to clean your hands and face with a Lysol® wipe. He's quick and gentle.

Each time he wipes my face, I close my eyes. The sky is dark and it's raining blueberries. Grape juice floods the streets.

But like all storms, it will pass.

Day 8

I'M DOING THE online dating thing and matched with a princess today. She said she likes long walks on an empty beach with six feet of separation.

Meet you there, I replied back.

We excitedly ran up to our tiny sandcastle on the beach. Her blue mask matches her royal dress. My white rubber gloves are custom made for a prince.

But the government has put the castle on lockdown and we cannot enter. So, we just sit there in silent frustration with nothing to do but watch the tide come in.

The rising water floods the place and, not long after, the tide erodes the castle and her away.

Day 9

PUT ON MY shoes and went for a stroll today. Checked myself out in the mirror first to make sure I looked semi-human.

Removed a piece of raw meat stuck between my fangs.

Trotting down the sidewalk, I approached a stranger also out for some fresh air. When we got closer, he sneezed into his elbow and I immediately thought, *Great. Now we're both infected.*

As we walked past each other we nodded hello and I noticed a large mustard stain on his jogging pants.

I wondered...regular or Dijon?

When I got home, I took off my shoes and sat back down on my couch. *Maybe it was hot mustard?* I thought to myself.

Damnit, now I won't be able to sleep tonight.

Day 10

WOKE UP THIS morning to blue skies and sunshine. The world can't end today – it's way too nice out!

But, just in case, I secretly buried a duffle bag filled with McDonald's coupons in a park.

On my seventh birthday, my mother organized a party at McDonald's and I got to meet my idol, Ronald McDonald. He was all smiles and full of life as I watched him come to me, walking across a pool of colorful balls.

If the world ever does catch fire, I have faith he'll come to my rescue.

He kicks down my apartment door and lifts me up off my couch, carrying me like a baby, back to the motherland.

Feed me french fries and tell me everything will be okay, just like you've done a billion times before.

Day 11

GET UP, PUT on pants, sleep, repeat. During isolating times like these ones, routine is important.

My choice of pants during the pandemic is the classic jogger. Ultra-relaxed, easily washable and camo in color. I have three pairs.

My confused jeans now sit in the back of my closet wondering what's going on.

I picture a bloated President Donald Trump in a pair of joggers isolating at his Mar-a-Lago carnival funhouse. He sits in a red velvet throne with a pet alligator close by. Everything is painted red and gold. The place smells like mold.

Every morning at dawn, I raise a pair of camo joggers up a flagpole on the roof of my own tiny kingdom. They flap strongly in the wind, symbolizing I'm still here. And every night, I take them down.

Routine is important.

Day 12

I'VE TURNED INTO a house cat as I spend most of my days staring out a window. I watch people walk by, dressed as bandits with their masks and gloves on.

If you were ever going to rob a bank, I would assume now would be the time to do it.

Vacant parks across the city look like crime scenes as playgrounds have been taped off by the authorities. No humans allowed.

But I'm not a human anymore.

I'm a big lazy cat who just wants to jump on your lap and snuggle. Maybe tonight I'll head over to the playground and poop in the sandbox.

As I continue to stare out the window, I daydream about my new and exciting life. A fury bandit in the night, being chased around by animal control.

Day 13

OVER THE WEEKEND, I baked a delicious and massive chocolate chip banana bread. Not to brag, but it's so big, it barely fits in my apartment.

After posting a boomerang video of it on my social media, I sliced it open with a chainsaw and crawled inside.

Life full-time in the baked good feels like a slice of heaven. I feel safe and protected from the outside infected world. You could sneeze and cough all over it and it wouldn't make the slightest difference to me.

It's like I've returned back to the womb.

I'm starting to gain weight but if that's the worst thing to happen to me during this pandemic, I'm pretty damn lucky.

Although, I'm pretty sure when all this is over, my body will be discovered in the loaf like Han Solo in frozen carbonate. I've posted the recipe link in my Instagram bio, just in case you cared.

Day 14

THE WORLD HEALTH Organization recommends that the average adult do 30 minutes of physical activity each day.

One of their suggestions is dancing to music.

My first slow dance with a girl was in grade six. Her name was Alison Harvey and it happened at a party in my friend's basement.

I got three dances in before the basement lights flickered off and on by my friend's mother at the top of the stairs. It was her way of signalling that the party was over without having to awkwardly come down.

As I dance alone in my apartment now, I wait for the lights to flicker again, letting me know when the pandemic is over and I can leave. But in the meantime, I do the moonwalk.

Straight into your heart.

Day 15

AS MOTHER NATURE slowly heals herself, we anxiously wait and tend to the sick.

The saviour of our sanity is a tattooed redneck who once walked across the South with a tiger entourage but now sits caged like us.

His following grows each day, keeping busy making signs and T-shirts. They identify each other by their tiger print blouses and freshly trimmed mullets.

Believe in him or not.

Looking down on earth, the collective glow from our television sets broadcasting his sermons form the face of a menacing tiger. Soon, he will be released again and Mother Nature will roar.

All hail the Tiger King.

Day 16

THE ONE THING I'm losing control over in this quarantine life is the volume of dirty dishes pilling up in my apartment.

Cheap rent = no dishwasher.

I moved into this apartment seven years ago. My landlord was an old Greek man, who not only owned the low-rise building, but lived in it with his lovely wife whom he was married to for over fifty years.

I only knew him for three months before he passed away from leukemia.

But sitting in my apartment today, if I hold a dirty plate up to my ear and listen very closely, I can still hear him telling stories of his younger days living in Greece.

The days when nobody had a dishwasher, so everyone had to stick together to pull through.

Day 17

HOW MANY TIMES have I washed my hands today? I've lost count.

My soap of choice is a Dove® bar. Moisturizes and kills germs at the same time. As backup, I've got Irish Spring® and something called Hydra Bliss in a bottle.

Way in the back of my medicine cabinet covered in dust, you'll find some kind of witchcraft brew from 1807. It's like this green liquid syrup and one of the ingredients is a tooth from a young boy.

My neighbours above me sing "Purple Rain" by Prince while washing their hands. A power ballad about the end of the world that combines rock, R&B, gospel and orchestral music.

Every morning, I wake in an anxious silence...and then Prince comes and saves the day.

Day 18

MY BARBER SHOP is closed. I am forced to cut my own hair.

For the majority of my adult life, I've always had a healthy set of dark, thick hair. But these days, it's starting to thin and get greyer.

As I took an electric razor to my head today, I watched the hair fall into my bathroom sink. When all was said and done, not a bad job. A hidden talent perhaps.

Instead of throwing the hair out, I've decided to keep it as a memento for when the pandemic is finally over.

Who knows? Maybe I'll open my own barbershop. I'll replace the outside barber's pole with my bag of hair, like mistletoe.

Kiss underneath and live forever.

Day 19

I'M PRETTY SURE the monster under my bed is infected. It won't stop sneezing.

When I was a kid, I used to walk down into my childhood basement with the lights off and stand there alone in the dark until my body would get flushed with intense fear. Then I'd race back up the stairs before some monster could grab my little leg and drag me back down.

I think when these social isolating days are over, I'll return for a visit and let the monster catch me this time.

*Cue sitcom theme song

Cut to a smiling me and my new bestie holding hands while we skip towards a park. We joyfully throw yellow caution tape into the sky. In today's episode, we discover that the monster's name is Zordo and that his favourite thing to eat is dirty socks.

And the lesson I learned is that the more I know about it, the less I fear.

Day 20

WHEN I WAS a kid, I was a massive Michael Jordan fan and I wanted to be just like him.

I had the shoes, the jersey and a framed poster of him that hung above my bed. In it, he is photographed mid-flight as he effortlessly soars towards the basket.

Nobody has been in the sky like that since.

I harassed my parents to buy me a basketball net and eventually they caved. In grade eight, I made the school team. I wanted the jersey with number 23 on it but our team captain had first dibs. His name was Joe Masse and boy, he could dunk! I couldn't even touch the rim.

I think that season I scored two points. After winning six championships, MJ retired and so did I. I took down my poster and hung up my jersey for good.

I still think about trying to touch that rim. And in my COVID fever dreams, I'm about to take off.

Day 21

WENT INTO MY laundromat this afternoon wearing jeans to wash my jogging pants.

The owner is a tiny old Asian lady whose pockets are always filled with loose change. But like a ghost, she's never there. She only appears if you summon her because of an issue. In order to summon her, you must toss a coin in a washing machine and say her name three times. She then emerges from out of a dryer.

My issue today was the quarantine blues.

So I tossed a coin, called out her name and she appeared before me. We then held hands and jumped into a washer filled with warm soapy water and spun around all afternoon in a ferris wheel of tiny bubbles.

Feed me a Tide Pod and tell me you love me.

Day 22

THE BAT SIGNAL turns on and an image of a rubber glove is projected high into the night sky. A surgical gown is quickly slipped on, face shield mounted, gloved hand clenched into a fist.

A new superhero rises in our city.

From the rooftop of a hospital, a nurse sits perched and ready to fight as the evil villain Doctor COVID threatens world domination.

Every evening at 7:30PM sharp, citizens lean out their windows and bang their pots and pans as loudly as they can, like a rally cry.

It's our new national anthem. And it beats to the heart of our brave hero.

Day 23

I OWN AN Oculus Quest. It's a virtual reality headset that allows me to safely travel around.

Recently, alone in my apartment, I sang "Happy Birthday" to a random grandmother who just turned 100 years old. It was her first time in VR and I was a robot.

Hosted by her grandson, the outdoor patio party was filled with colourful balloons, a cake and even a bouncy castle.

As cheerful robots came up and hugged her, I remember thinking what a different and surreal world this must be for her to live through.

We have nothing in common, except I know how she feels.

Day 24

TODAY IS MY Dad's 75th birthday. Normally, our family would meet up and celebrate with dinner and cake.

My dad is great and loves to crack jokes. He's a devoted husband and a chemist at heart. He even flew jets in the Canadian Air Force. As a teenager, he was the recipient of the Queen's Scout Award. It's the highest youth award achievable in the Commonwealth scouting organization.

✵ ✵ ✵

Now retired, my dad spends his days fixing things around the house and just finished season three of Ozark.

He's my commander-in-chief and I'm honoured to be his son. Happy Birthday, Dad.

Wish I was there.

Day 25

I HAVE A new neighbour who just moved in a few months ago.

She's an actress who gets typecast in commercials, always playing a young professional who starts each morning right with a Starbucks coffee.

She's also the neighbourhood's face mask dealer.

For twelve bucks, she'll meet you in a dark alleyway and sell you a decorative mask made of 100% cotton.

She operates out of her apartment and the other night, I dreamt that she got raided by a SWAT team wearing their own protective masks. She came out in handcuffs covered in rubber bands and pieces of polyester fabric, charged with counterfeiting and fraud.

As I put on my face mask for the very first time, I start to feel different. I look in the mirror and I don't recognize myself. I wonder how long that feeling will last. Or is this the new me?

I suddenly need my Starbucks coffee fix.

Day 26

YESTERDAY, I HAD a virtual movie night with my good friend, Johnny. We watched *Braveheart*. It's one of those nostalgic movies we have bonded over since the 90s.

I first met Johnny in my grade six class. He was a competitive swimmer. Tall and talented, he destroyed provincial records.

Every morning since then, he's continued to get up at the crack of down to jump into a pool. His competitive days are long gone but he started his own swim club for kids, turning himself into a full-time coach.

When these social isolating days are finally over, I picture Johnny in blue face paint with the rest of his tiny tribe of swimmers charging towards a pool. He yells, "freeeedom!" as they cannonball into it.

He then slowly sinks to the bottom, letting the water heal his hard-fought battle wounds.

Day 27

I'M DEFINITELY SPENDING too much time on my couch, so I just ordered some home exercise equipment.

Not long ago, I used to be an active member at my local gym. I would go in four- to five-times a week over the course of a year. It felt like a second home.

The manager was a young guy named Ivan. He was meek but built like a tank, and always had a protein powder moustache.

We chit chatted here and there and got to know each other over time. Towards the end of that year, he offered me a full-time personal trainer position if I wanted it. I entertained the amusing idea for a few days before politely declining.

As I sit on my couch with my membership on hold, waiting for my equipment to arrive, I picture Ivan in a FedEx outfit showing up at my door. We catch up for a few minutes until I sign for the delivery and tip him generously.

New job. Same old protein powder moustache.

Day 28

WITH EVERYONE FORCED to stay home with nothing to do, I'm sure there will be a COVID baby boom.

When I was a teenager, I took a babysitting course. We learned things like CPR and how to change a diaper. I remember taking our final exam and when the instructor wasn't looking, everyone would immaturely throw things at each other and giggle.

After barely passing the course, I quickly became my neighbourhood's go-to babysitter for $20 a night. My favourite part of those babysitting days was relaxing on a neighbour's couch with a big bag of chips and a cold pop after putting restless children to bed.

From deep in my closet, I proudly pull out my framed certificate and blow off the dust as a diaper shaped sun slowly begins to rise, soon to be the dawn of a new day.

Day 29

TODAY I WATCHED a single rubber glove fly high in the sky, carried by the wind.

The city is littered with them.

The mayor has called in a special task force to handle the situation. Under the cover of their face masks and the darkness of the night, the elite team silently combs past your home. Half-human, half-machine, they are marked by an image of a purple glove on their bare backs.

Immune from the virus, they freely travel from city to city and any sighting of them is extremely rare. If you're lucky enough to spot one, legend already has it good fortune will come your way.

So your mission is to follow the glove in the wind, to treasures and beyond.

Day 30

I HAD MY first Zoom dance party last night from my computer. My background image was a picture of me when I was eight years old.

The party was hosted by DJ Purell, who wore a giant afro wig and was dressed as Jesus. My speakers blared his techno hymns as I did the worm across my kitchen floor.

The other twelve partygoers on my screen were his social media followers who praised each beat that he played. "If you haven't danced at a Zoom party, did you even quarantine?!" they shouted his message at me.

I got down on my knees and invited his electronic music into my digital heart. As the base dropped, the new age began.

And on the 29th day of the pandemic, I saw the LED light.

Day 31

I WALKED INTO my local convenience store to buy some peanut butter and a bag of chips. You were already there, holding a blue Powerade.

The clock struck midnight as a chocolate bar fell to the floor in slow motion.

With our face masks on, we danced around each other like at a masquerade ball. We both reached out and grabbed the same bag of chips and when our bare hands touched, for that split second, time stood still.

I envisioned us in the future sharing your blue Powerade. The pandemic no longer.

I wanted to pay for your snacks but I had to keep my distance. So instead, I just watched you pay and exit the store. You walked up the empty street and disappeared into the dark. I left a trail of chip crumbs leading back to my place.

That's where you'll find me and my peanut butter-filled heart.

Day 32

I WAS ON a walk today when I saw an old man sitting outside on his front porch, a big and beautiful white parrot in a cage beside him.

"Don't touch your face," it squawked at me.

I wasn't sure how to react. I thought about laughing it off or replying with a friendly comment like, "I sure won't!" or "Thanks for the reminder."

I also wondered, did the old man teach the bird to say that or did the bird naturally pick it up in the house? The old man winked at me and I could tell he wasn't going to tell me his secret.

I pictured him waking up the next day, the severed head of the parrot lying next to him in bed.

I laughed sinisterly at the thought, intentionally loud enough for him to hear. Now we both had secrets as I continued on my walk.

Day 33

I LIVE ALONE, so lately I've been starting to crave more human interaction.

Yesterday, I got an automated call congratulating me that I won a free cruise. It reminded me of a news article I read back in 2011 about a fire on a Carnival cruise that stranded the ship at sea for days, resulting in passengers being forced to poop in plastic bags.

As I called the number back, I pictured going on my winning trip with my scammer. Together, we board the ship and excitedly wave at the seagulls in the sky.

I ended up getting an answering machine, where at the sound of the beep, I left my name and social insurance number.

I also mentioned that whatever happens, I've got enough bags to hold their poop, always and forever.

Day 34

ORDERED SOME GROCERIES online and drove to Walmart yesterday to pick them up.

As I waited in my car, I saw a massive line of people outside slowly entering the super store but strangely, no one coming out.

Just past the rubber hoses and men's shoes in aisle 48, I pictured customers entering a secret portal leading to another dimension. A twilight zone-esque place called "Jacksonville, Florida" where beaches are open and people high-five with no gloves on.

Eventually, the young Walmart employee came out with my order. After placing the bags in my car, I tried to generously tip him but he politely refused my money.

He walked back to the store, thinking about warm sand between his toes.

Day 35

FROM MY WINDOW, I watch a gang of raccoons march down an empty street like they own the place now.

A few years ago, a raccoon briefly lived inside my ceiling. We used to sing love songs to each other late at night. After the critter stayed five nights without paying rent, my landlord called animal control and a guy named Tad showed up with his van of booby traps.

When I first met Tad, I noticed he had a glass eye. An old work-related injury. It didn't take long for him to find the secret tiny entrance to my apartment and he sealed it forever shut with steel wire fencing.

I look back out my window and I hear the leader of the raccoon gang call out for Tad. They got a bone to pick. And maybe another eye.

Day 36

LAST NIGHT, I had a dream that I was in the future.

I was shopping in a Whole Foods when someone sneezed. The person was immediately strung up on a cross and customers threw overpriced tomatoes at them.

Angry protests broke out around the world. People wore face masks and held up signs that read, "The Devil loves a Sneezer!" and "Death to the sneeze!"

I woke up drenched in sweat.

I took a walk in a public place and sneezed into my elbow. Nobody was around to hear it, so I sneezed again, louder than ever before.

Day 37

YESTERDAY, I SAW a paper plane flying high in the sky. It was bright orange with the phrase "hang tight" scrawled across it in crayon.

This morning, I saw another one depart from a hospital window. Written on it was a love letter from a sick man missing his wife.

"Come fly the COVID-free skies with Air Purell," says the commercial on my pirate radio.

I picture myself sitting in the folded plane and getting handed a mini bottle of hand sanitizer. "That'll be forty dollars," the smiling attendant says. I pull out my wallet, hoping they take Monopoly money.

As the international skies begin to clear around the world, more and more paper planes begin to take flight. All those tiny hopes and dreams, racing through the clouds.

Day 38

IT'S A SATURDAY, which means I'm cleaning my apartment.

My disinfectant of choice is the Comet cleaner with bleach. A trusted household brand and World Health Organization-approved.

The label on the back of the bottle says it contains calcium hydroxide and, if swallowed under the direction of any president, to call the poison control center.

I picture the poison control center as an underground bunker. Inside the bare cement room sits a steel office desk with a rotary phone on it. Napping daily at the desk for the past fifty years is an eighty-eight-year-old employee named Elmer. Covered in dust, he wears a big yellow authoritative badge and can't remember the last time he's ever picked up that phone.

But third caller in wins a free shirt that says, "I'm with stupid!"

Day 39

YESTERDAY AFTERNOON, I drove out to visit my parents for the first time in months. We stayed in the backyard and planned to keep six feet apart at all times.

My parents live in a quiet gated retirement community, where my mom enjoys her Aquafit classes and my dad's best friend is named Brian.

At one point during my visit, Brian and his wife Dorothy randomly showed up. Dorothy talked about her worried daughter constantly coming over to drop off expensive organic food. Not wanting her elderly parents to venture out to the grocery store and risk getting sick, she surely must have disapproved of me, a stranger from the big city, sitting with them.

At the end of my visit, my mom caved and broke the rules, giving me a hug goodbye as my dad watched from a distance, shaking his head.

She squeezed tightly, hoping the love between a mother and her son is bigger than this universe, immune to anything.

Day 40

I WATCHED A YouTube clip of a funeral that took place in an online video game. A community of gamers came together to pay tribute to a beloved member who passed away in real life from COVID complications.

It reminded me of a time, four years ago, when a good friend brought me over to his neighbour's basement to show me his impressive collection of over twenty pinball machines.

Both my friend and his neighbour were part of a pinball league.

The bright lights and ringing sounds were overwhelming and I felt like I was in a casino operated by Willy Wonka. I pictured my friend's neighbour making his grand entrance by sliding down the basement banister in a purple velvet suit and top hat. Singing about the excitement of swallowing a little shiny metallic ball, allowing you to play forever.

"This is the basement of arcade dreams and unlimited lives," he sings a lyric from his song. A place to come and forget about all the troubles in the world.

Day 41

BEFORE I WAS allowed into my local grocery store yesterday, security questioned me if I had any flu like symptoms.

The leader of the security team is an extremely large man with a baby face named Paul. Outside of the store, he's been standing strong like a Queen's Guard since day one of the pandemic.

Yesterday was a new question though, and it caught me off guard. Previously, he always asked if I had travelled outside of the country in the past two weeks. I always replied no, tempted to ask if he knew of any flight deals.

When this pandemic is over, I'm going to miss the guardian of our grocery store and his safety-related questions. I wonder if I'll ever see him again.

I doubt it. But I like to think wherever he'll travel to next, he'll always be protecting a grocery store somewhere out there. Warning customers of any aisle spills, standing guard for thee.

Day 42

I WENT FOR a walk this morning. Checked myself out in the mirror first to make sure I looked semi-human.

Noticed my claws are getting longer.

I decided to trot through an alleyway to avoid any human contact but immediately ran into another person with the same idea. I attempted a friendly hello but accidentally howled instead. The person smiled, exposing their fangs.

It was like looking into a mirror as we slowly circled each other, sniffing each other's scent. We then abruptly got spooked by an incoming car and quickly ran off in opposite directions.

When I got back to the comfort of my stale apartment, I could still smell fresh human on me; this wild odour, full of excitement and feelings. Craving to meet again, I'll have to take another walk tomorrow.

Until then, I sit in my cage.

Day 43

TOM HANKS HAS donated his blood and plasma to help with the vaccine research.

In my pandemic dream last night, I imagined a world where a vaccine from his blood was produced. Once administered, a side effect was that you would temporarily morph into a random Tom Hanks character from any one of his movies.

To mark the end of the pandemic, humanity celebrated by launching a box of chocolates into outer space with the recorded soundbite, "Life is like a box of chocolates: you never know what you're gonna get" forever on repeat.

And it was in my deepest cycle of my REM sleep that I followed those treats out into the cold and black abyss, comforted only by the voice of Tom Hanks, the man with the sweetest heart.

Day 44

INSTEAD OF MY usual home cooking today, I grabbed takeout to help support my local restaurants. One of my fave joints is an Indian restaurant called Banjara.

The owner is a short man named Gupil. His hair has an orange tint to it, similar to the colour of the two kitchen fires the restaurant had last summer.

Entering the restaurant, I am greeted by a giant plastic container of hand sanitizer that looks like it was possibly brewed in the basement. I make sure I thoroughly clean my hands first before I approach the counter and say hi to the cute cashier, who I've had a crush on since I first ordered butter chicken from her five years ago.

As I leave the restaurant with my order, I picture her and I getting married after the pandemic. On the rooftop of Banjara, high up in the sky, we stand before Gupil. She looks like an Indian princess; my hair is slicked back with hand sanitizer, and our love is on fire.

Day 45

I COULD DEFINITELY use a drink right about now.

My favourite local cocktail bar, Civil Liberties, is temporarily closed. It's a place where everyone once knew my name.

When they first opened five years ago, for a brief time they had a specialty drink. They would cut a pineapple in half, fill it with shaved ice, rum and a variety of other liquors. Then they would stick a large straw in it and light the fruit on fire. It was something you would expect to drink in the middle of the afternoon, in a pee-filled pool, at an all-inclusive vacation resort.

As all the pools in the Caribbean slowly begin to filter out the urine and rejuvenate back to its natural chlorine balance, I wonder how long it will take for humans to pee in them again once the pandemic is over.

To find the answer, you must dance naked around the sacred pineapple and ask the spirit of the rum.

Day 46

YESTERDAY THE WEATHER was perfect and everyone was out enjoying it. I live next to a city park, so my sunny afternoon was spent watching people-watching at a safe distance from my balcony.

I watched an athletic family of six jog together in single file. They moved quickly and in sync, each proudly showing off their brand new and matching fanny packs.

I witnessed a middle-aged man dressed like a teenager zip past on a skateboard.

At one point, I watched a twenty-something girl walk aimlessly around wearing a pair of bright neon green socks. With her pale arms folded across her chest, she looked like she was struggling to remember how to enjoy herself.

The socks were a good first start. A tiny beacon of neon green light, shining a message of optimism and hope. She'll never get lost in the shadows of the park, not with those things on, guiding her down the right path.

Day 47

OKAY, SO NOW we have murder hornets?! I wonder how many newly formed rap groups or death metal bands will be calling themselves that next year.

The other day, I went over to my sister's for a socially distanced backyard visit. I stopped at a donut shop first to pick up some donuts for my nephews. Jack likes the maple kind and Chase likes the ones with rainbow-coloured sprinkles.

When I arrived in the backyard, I found a bored Jack with his bow and arrow. He's been sorely missing his friends, so when he saw me show up holding a box of donuts, his head almost exploded.

His favourite game to play is Monster. The rules are simple: I pretend I'm a monster and chase him around the yard. If I catch him, I eat him up like a tasty treat. A few times he screamed as I got close but, in the end, he survived.

As the sun went down, the maple-faced boy with his bow and arrow watched the defeated donut monster drive away in a Toyota Yaris with an arrow pierced into the back bumper. Hopefully tomorrow will bring a new adventure. Bring on the murder hornets.

Day 48

THERE'S A BASEBALL diamond in my local park that has the name "Steve" spray-painted in large letters on the protective fencing behind home plate.

A last name would have been helpful.

I know many Steves now and have known many Steves in my life. Currently, there are two at my work. A third Steve recently quit a few months back and even had the same last name as one of our current Steves. I'm not making this up.

As for the Steve at the baseball diamond, maybe it's the name of the person last season who hit the winning homerun in the championship game? I'm picturing him now, stuck at home, lying on a couch, still daydreaming about that moment.

This year, the league has sadly suspended the season. But Steve will be back again one day, his name shining in the bright lights.

Day 49

I BOUGHT A bicycle yesterday. I'd started getting bored of my walks and eventually lost all motivation to go on them. Plus, now I can jump over strangers instead of awkwardly walking around them.

My local bike shop is a block away and the owner is a guy named Angelo who has an easygoing personality. His favourite things in life are cash deals and free tune-ups.

It's been ages since I last owned a bike. I remember my first bike had a banana seat and the neighbourhood kids made fun of me as I rode around. Looking at old photos of myself back then, I also may or may not have had a bowl cut.

But look at me now!

I felt so cool riding my fancy new bike home yesterday and I can't wait for the summer weather that's around the corner. Maybe I'll return to my old childhood neighbourhood and pop a wheelie.

Day 50

THE 2020 PANDEMIC spring/summer fashion line is here!

I saw a man strutting down an empty street like it was his catwalk, wearing a bucket on his head, a garbage bag jacket, bubble wrap pants and astronaut boots.

Very COVID chic.

As the man disappeared around the corner, a woman made her modeling debut with a bathroom towel draped over her head. I asked from a social distance who she was wearing and she replied, "Bed, Bath and Beyond."

It's at the home décor store I found the exclusive after party, sponsored by Lysol. I gained access through the back door by whispering the password "liquid solutions". The man with the astronaut boots was there. He lay down on a soft bed and closed his tired eyes.

It's a lot of work to feel this safe.

Day 51

TODAY IS MOTHER'S Day and because of the pandemic, it's the first time in my life I won't be able to celebrate in person with my mom.

My French-Canadian mother is the sweetest woman you'll ever meet. She only stands at 5'4 but raised my sister and I with enormous love.

Now retired, my mom prefers YTV movies over Netflix and last year rented the entire *Game of Thrones* series on DVD from her local library. She watched with her own protective dire wolf, Sasha the Cat, closely sitting by.

Fun fact: If you stare at one of her homemade apple pies long enough, God's face will suddenly appear.

In these uncertain times filled with anxiety and depression, Mother's Day is now needed more than ever. In the next 24 hours, my heart beats stronger recognizing that my mom is inside it.

Day 52

THIS QUARANTINE HAS been happening for almost two months now and I still haven't picked up a new hobby or taken an online class in anything.

Maybe I'll try learning the saxophone again?

A few years ago, I walked into my local music store and rented an alto that came with the number of a neighbourhood teacher. Her name was Sara and she was a young Asian woman who lived with her boyfriend a few blocks away from me.

Two days later, I was in their apartment taking my first lesson. Sara and her boyfriend were in a jazz band together and it must have driven him crazy to listen to me in the other room butcher Twinkle Twinkle Little Star for an entire hour. After that, my own desire to play quickly faded and I never took a lesson again, probably to the relief of the boyfriend.

Just when he thought 2020 couldn't get any worse, I wonder if she's offering any online classes?

Day 53

MY FAVOURITE THING to do right now is ride the subway.

Entering the station, I'm always greeted by a creepy old man in the collector booth warning me to turn around before it's too late.

While I wait for my ride and stand on the platform with nobody around, I start to hear things. Whispers echoing all around me, saying things like, "Remember to keep a social distance between myself," and "Stand back behind the yellow line."

The yellow line that erodes away like all other human connections in this new pandemic life.

Eventually, the shiny metal snake pulls into the station, slowly opening its mouth for me as I cautiously step inside. Its breath smells like alcohol-based disinfectant spray.

As my ride begins to leave the station, I'm never sure where the next stop is and I keep my hands inside my pockets at all times.

Day 54

SINCE THE QUARANTINE has started, I've spent around 600 hours on my couch and counting.

This red two-seater of mine is large and super comfy. I got it ten years ago in a breakup with a long-term ex. She got the bed.

If you place a mini bottle of Purell under the couch cushion and take a nap, you'll be visited by the COVID fairy, who will wash your body clean while you dream of grocery stores with no lineups.

But if you offer an 8oz bottle with a hand pump, you'll be taken to a magical land filled to the brim with other couches. It's always here I build my fortress made of pillows and cushions.

There are no clocks to keep time, so wake me up when it's all over.

Day 55

WENT ON A walk today. Checked myself out in the mirror first to make sure I looked semi-human.

Tucked my furry tail back into my pants.

Walking past a row of neighbourhood houses with their windows open, I could smell from the sidewalk what each house was cooking for dinner. The first house had a vegetable beef stew broiling in a pot. The second house had dill salmon baking in the oven. But it was the third house that made me stop.

A secret family recipe was in the works here. I closed my eyes and this time, inhaled the heavy scent of spices and sauces deep into my lungs. This comforting home-cooked aroma instantly made me feel like I was part of their family, now standing outside like a distant relative who showed up unannounced.

In these risky and dangerous times, I've travelled so far from down the block.

Day 56

I WOKE UP this morning and read my daily horoscope. It said I should get off my couch and seize the day!

With peanut butter all over my face, I laughed out loud to myself.

A few years ago, I went and got a psychic reading from an old lady who lives in my neighbourhood. Her name is Neya and when I asked where she was originally from, she claimed to be hatched from a giant egg in outer space. Her husband was from Florida.

Staring into her crystal ball, she looked into the future and told me that one day planet Earth will stand still but I will find a way to make it spin again.

As I washed off the peanut butter that was caked on my face, I felt reborn. Hatched from a crystal ball, ready to seize the day.

Day 57

AS MORE AND more businesses slowly begin to reopen their doors to the public, I read that one American restaurant has seated mannequins at half their tables to support social distancing.

I hope you don't mind while they all watch you eat.

When I was a little kid, I used to watch an 80's television show called Today's Special. It was about a department store mannequin named Jeff that would come to life each night and hang out with his group of friends.

※ ※ ※

I'm picturing the sequel, where thirty years later, Jeff comes back to life and wonders where everybody is. Isolated, he roams around the department store for months desperately searching for any kind of social interaction. The final episode is about the store reopening with new social distancing measures in place, but Jeff has already turned back into a mannequin. Feeling frozen in time, forever changed.

Day 59

TODAY IN CANADA, it's Victoria Day, which is a national holiday celebrating the birthday of Queen Victoria that also marks the unofficial start of summer. If alive today, her majesty would be turning 201 years old.

Prime Minister Justin Trudeau jumps out of a Baskin Robbins ice cream cake with a rose in his mouth.

Our current Queen is self-isolating in her palace across the pond and I'm totally picturing her in Adidas track pants pulling out her perfect banana bread loaf from her giant-sized oven that is built from solid gold. Later, on a Zoom call with Meghan Markle, the Queen will show off her royal loaf saying, "this is how it's done."

As a few fireworks shoot up into the dark sky tonight, the sparkling light will expose a nation hunkered down in quarantine, where the only action happening is an ice cream-covered Justin Trudeau and his wife making sweet love, while Meghan Markle hangs up on the Queen.

Day 60

IN ALL THE pandemic lineups I've been in so far, the longest one I stood in happened two days ago outside of my local grocery store. It was about a twenty-minute wait to get inside.

The person directly in front of me was a young woman that was covered in cat hair and wore a large empty backpack. If I had to guess, the backpack was once used to carry university textbooks of subjects on astronomy. Only because she was on her phone the entire time reading an internet article on a recently discovered planet, located millions of lightyears away from here.

※ ※ ※

That, and her socks also had a galaxy print.

As I inched closer to the entrance of the building, I looked up into the sky and dreamt about this newly discovered planet. One that could be virus-free, where the only thing to worry about is if you're allergic to cat hair or not.

And then before I knew it, I was floating into the store.

Day 61

YESTERDAY, I MET up with a Craigslist stranger to purchase some home exercise equipment. "It'll be easy to spot me," I messaged the seller. "I'll be the guy in the fancy suit and top hat."

It had been awhile since I left my house.

I bought my fancy suit many years ago from a menswear boutique just down the street from me. The owner was a lovely lady named Willa, who had this amazing curly mop of red hair. Her store closed a year later and she left town, but to this day, you can still find single strands of her hair sticking to things around the neighbourhood.

As I sat in my car at the meeting point waiting for the Craigslist stranger to arrive, I noticed a curly red hair stuck to my suit jacket. It must have been a good luck charm, as the exchange went smoothly and I even got a discount on the ab roller!

Having the time of my pandemic life.

Day 62

THE OTHER DAY for the first time in this pandemic, I met up with a good friend.

It was her first time, as well.

She wanted to buy some plants for her condo, so I joined her on the walk over to the nursery making sure we kept a social distance with our face masks on. It was a beautiful day and the nursery was filled with a variety of different plants and flowers. It was a calming world to be in from the anxious one we were both used to.

On the way back, my friend asked if I wanted to come up and enjoy the sunset from her balcony, which sat 32 floors up into the sky. "Balcony only," I replied. "Balcony only," she repeated.

As the sun began to set, we watched from the top of the world and eventually held hands. We felt like two teenagers breaking the law as everything turned siren red. But for that brief yet comforting human moment, it was much needed. And then I washed my hands and drove home in the dark.

Day 63

AS YOU READ this, a new pair of jogging pants quickly travels past your home enroute to me. The emergency situation happened yesterday when a hole suddenly appeared in my favourite pair.

So the online order was made with a rush delivery.

The courier who carries my package was born in a distribution warehouse. Along with thousands of others, they emerged one-by-one from out of a womb-like oven, down a conveyor belt and straight into the arms of the God of Retail, who is short, bald, and sits on a high throne of plastic money. The courier, naked and cold, is then inspected for damage and stamped with a tracking number as its seal of approval.

The bigger the hole grows in my jogging pants, the more stuff I buy online. Eventually, I start to feel like a discarded courier, forever marked as a refund.

But then my new package arrives.

Day 64

WENT ON A bike ride this morning. Checked myself out in the mirror first to make sure I looked semi-human. Wiped the red winestache and clown makeup off my face.

Riding my bike down the street, I came across a house with two large opened suitcases stuffed with random things, laying on the edge of the front yard. A small hand-written note attached said "free for the taking". Perhaps this was the aftermath of a COVID spring cleaning? Or maybe a recent divorce?

Rooting through the used items, I reached deep into the suitcase and pulled out a VHS tape from the old blockbuster days. The movie was Groundhog Day. Starring the hilarious Bill Murray, it's about a man who relives the same day over and over again, bringing him to the edge of insanity.

I could use some more comedy in my life right now, so I rode away empty handed.

Day 65

AS MANY BUSINESSES permanently close down during the pandemic, Disney World recently announced plans to reopen soon but have yet to set a date.

When I was a kid, my family visited Disney World and I remember meeting Mickey. I was super shy, but he was a charmer. A true character of class, who gently brought me out from hiding behind my mom and sweet talked me into giving him a high-five. The trip was the highlight of my childhood, even though later that day I puked all over myself after eating a corn dog.

All these years later, I imagine a frantic Mickey in the basement of the Magic Kingdom working tirelessly to help find a COVID vaccine. Test trials have already begun on Pluto and Goofy.

Believe in a vaccine or not but Disney World is the most magical place on earth, where corn dogs disappear and reappear right before your eyes.

Day 66

AFTER OVER TWO months of quarantine isolation, I'm thankful that summer weather has finally arrived. I've officially shed my jogging pants (like a snake shedding its skin) and switched over to shorts.

Transition to greatness!

My shorts of choice are the flat front style with the inseam pull-on for class and comfort. They are also stain-resistant, which is key, especially with my recent addiction to homemade nacho cheese. My backup pair is the cargo short. They come with extra-large pockets that currently hold six bottles of my cheesy brew. They are also my survival pair, just in case shit hits the fan and I need to quickly hit the road.

You never know this summer. A park full of thousands of humans not social distancing could suddenly turn into a deadly herd of covidiots.

Day 67

THE ONE THING I'm definitely missing right now (and will for the rest of the year) is the movie theatre. That dark room, buttery popcorn and big screen.

It's the holy trinity.

The last movie I saw in theatres was *1917.* Set during the first world war, it follows two young soldiers who have to cross deep into enemy territory in order to deliver a lifesaving message to a regiment on a doomed mission. Not the same as watching something like that on my laptop.

Isolated during this pandemic, everything has shrunk down to a laptop size including my family, friends and co-workers. Now playing on my couch: this strange little movie called life.

Day 68

ONE OF MY best friends and his wife just had a baby boy.

I've known Dave since high school. We bonded over playing video games in his parent's basement.

Since those teenage days, Dave has grown into a delightful man. He's definitely the smartest, funniest and most thoughtful person I know. He also works hard at two jobs, is a fair landlord who owns multiple properties and is a loving father to his four-year-old daughter.

I'm not sure what the state of things will be when his daughter and son grow up, but knowing people like him exist in this world, I'm hopeful the future generation will be a source of brighter light. Finally emerging from out of this dark unfinished basement that we are still living in.

Day 69

I LIVE NEXT to a large city park and every now and again, a local man will enter it and start to sing at the top of his lungs.

His tenor voice is great and it booms across the empty, wooded land, definitely confusing the wildlife.

For the rest of us neighbouring humans who live surrounding the park, he's like our community messenger as his singing lets us know how we are doing during this pandemic battle. Songs in his bass range signify when someone has passed. His songs in falsetto express hope and alert us when government cheques have arrived in the mail.

But the pitch perfect song I'm excitedly anticipating, is his farewell swan song. I imagine him afterwards getting showered with face masks and roses, before disappearing forever into the cheering crowd.